Stream of Consciousness:
Poetics of the Universal

Peter Wuteh Vakunta

Langaa Research & Publishing CIG
Mankon, Bamenda

Publisher:
Langaa RPCIG
Langaa Research & Publishing Common Initiative Group
P.O. Box 902 Mankon
Bamenda
North West Region
Cameroon
Langaagrp@gmail.com
www.langaa-rpcig.net

Distributed in and outside N. America by African Books Collective
orders@africanbookscollective.com
www.africanbookscollective.com

ISBN: 9956-792-94-2

DISCLAIMER
All views expressed in this publication are those of the author and do
not necessarily reflect the views of Langaa RPCIG.

Dedication

For Global Citizens

Table of Contents

Preface

Poetry has the potential to serve as a double-edged weapon. In *Stream of Consciousness: Poetics of the Universal*, Vakunta stirs the hornet's nest, calls a spade a spade and throws gibes at emasculators of social justice. Vakunta refuses to sit on the fence and watch the world go by. Strong in the conviction that poets must adjudicate upon the affairs of men, the poet picks up the cudgels to do battle with forces of evil the world over. He gives to Caesar what is Caesar's and to God what is God's. Widely traveled and seasoned by his worldly experience, the poet serves the reader with a bitter-sweet menu analogous with the ontological labyrinth to which he has been exposed in the course of his peregrinations around the globe. In this anthology of poems spanning a quarter century, Vakunta bemoans the fate of a world where miscreants pass for holier-than-thous; wherein scoundrels speak for the voiceless; and mammon dines with servants of God. The portrait painted in this book is that of a world where moral bankrupts proceed with nauseating impunity to trample on the rights of lesser beings. *Stream of Consciousness: Poetics of the Universal* is the poet's loud cry against the reign of impunity and the endemic moral crisis that has become the canker of this blighted planet.

x

I. Man and Mortality

Stream of Consciousness

It's no light comment on our country
To say that we openly and consciously
Condone a system in which race
Determines who breathes
And who should not breathe,
Whom we execute and
Whom we set free!

Take a walk down memory lane—
Revisit the slaying of the black boy named
Trayvon Martin in Sanford Florida,
Recall the killing of yet another black boy
By the name of Michael Brown
By a trigger-happy policeman
In Ferguson in the State of Missouri

Remember the murder of the black man,
Eric Garner of Staten Island
By chokehold police tactics in New York
Don't forget the assassination of twelve-year old
Tamir Rice wielding a plastic gun by yet another
Vampire in police uniform in Cleveland!

It is now true as it has been
In the past that race makes or mars in
This land of the free!
The Supreme Court has
Acknowledged that race continues
To play a major role in capital punishment;
Yet has decided to ignore it,

For all intents and purposes.

This form of inhumane penalty
Has become the fate of black folks
A black person killing a white
Person in Oklahoma, Mississippi,
Virginia, Arkansas or North Carolina
Is more likely to get a death sentence
Than a white man killing a black man.

Racism has become so deep-rooted
In our psyche that it has now acquired
The veneer of normalcy!
Racism is enmeshed in daily parlance,
It is everywhere in commercials,
It is buried in institutional practices,
The school system has been re-segregated,

Racism is pervasive in messages in the workplace,
In social circles and everywhere
The more racism becomes invisible,
The easier it is for perpetrators to go scot-free!
Yesterday, Civil Rights Icon, Rosa Parks said, 'I'm tired.'
Today, she would say, 'I'm fed up!'

Rogue Cops

Flat foot,
Mange-mille,
Mbéré-Khaki,[1]
We buy the fatigues for you,
We buy the gun for you
To protect us day and night;
You take the gun and shoot us!

Rogue cop,
You kill our kids,
You rob our banks,
You deflower our daughters,
You harass the innocent.
Racial profiling is your stock-in-trade.
We're sick and tired of your roguery!

Casket

Had I known
That one day I will return
To dust as naked as an earth worm,
I wouldn't be so supercilious.

Had I known
That in death there are no greater beings,
And that we're all in the same boat,
I wouldn't be so vainglorious.

Had I known
That there's no room in the grave
For my ill-gotten wealth,
I wouldn't be so materialistic.

Had I known
That in Paradise there are no lesser races,
God is color blind,
I wouldn't be such a racist.

Had I known
That death makes no distinction
Between chiefs and nchindas[2],
I wouldn't be such a megalomaniac.

I now know that
Death is an equalizer;
It comes to all and sundry
In the same manner— Slumber in a casket.

Demise

Lying in state,
Hemmed in by a wall of obscurity
As dark as pitch,
I wish I could catch a glimpse
Of bona fide and phony mourners,
Alas, blind as a bat I am.

Lying in state,
As stiff as ramrod,
I long to hear sympathizers—
Lamentation and disparagement,
Alas, deaf as billows I am.

Lying in state,
Awaiting internment in the valley below,
I long to stir—
In mock attempt to undo my demise,
Alas, still as a log I am.

Pyrrhic Victory

Kill! Kill! Kill!
Tis the spirit of the bayonet,
Blood makes grass grow.
What makes grass green?
Blood! Blood! More blood!
Victory starts here!

Methinks ours is
A Pyrrhic victory—
One too costly to be of
Any real use to us,
We may know all our
Reassuring code-names—

Operation Enduring Justice;
Operation Just Cause;
Operation Desert Storm;
Operation Iraqi Freedom…
We'll never know the names
Of all compatriots killed for freedom.

Dawn of Darkness

[In memory of my beloved mother,
Nah Monica Mbiayuh who passed on in July 2006]

The sun has set under our roof.
It has set in our hearts.
Darkness, darkness, everywhere!
Nah Mbiah is no more!
Where's she gone to?
A journey of no return!
Nah Mbiah is no more!

You cannot know
The value of a mother until
You find the house without a mother.
You cannot feel the absence of maternal love
Until you find the house of a mother
Bereft of a dear mother,
Nah Mbiah is no more!

You cannot see the worth of a mother
More excellent than gold,
Until you find the mother's house
Empty of the mother,
Then you cry, and cry and cry.
Then you lament, and lament and lament,
Nah Mbiah is no more!

How do you mourn a beloved mother?
You pace and pace, up and down,
In the heart of darkness,

Seeking to find a departed mother,
But finding none, you turn away
To shed a flood of peppery tears,
Nah Mbiah is no more!

Nah, you've left us to our own devices,
Who'll cook food for us?
Nah, now that you have left us,
Who will cuddle us?
Nah, now that you are no more,
Who'll wash our dirty linen?

Oh,   Nah!
Nah, now that your eyes are closed,
Who'll watch over us?
We can't believe you are no more!
If wishes were horses,
We'll still have our mother here.
Alas, the hand of death is mighty!

Farewell

[Memorial poem for Brother,
David Wombong Vakunta Who
left us in June 2001 to meet the Lord]

Your terrestrial journey
Has come to an end, albeit too soon.
Had mortals a say in God's design,
Siblings would have wished
Your terrestrial sojourn longer,
Long enough to immortalize
Yourself through procreation.
Alas, Divine verdict brooks no appeal.

Our broken hearts bleed,
Our inundated eyes weep,
Myriad of questions without answers.
What really happened?
What went so horribly wrong?
Brother, who'll answer us?
God alone harbors
Answers to these queries.

You took leave without farewell!
Beloved brother—
Our wounded hearts are hard to heal.
When shall we see you again?
When shall we meet you again?
When shall we talk to you again?
We miss you dearly.
Farewell Dave!

Adieu Mother!

[Memorial poem for my beloved
mother-in-law, Veronica Mogho,
 who died on March 19, 2002]

Mother of one,
Mother of all,
How can we forget you
Beloved mother of
Many a son and daughter?
Some biological, others adopted.

Beloved mother,
Your altruism
Knew no bounds,
Your patience elastic,
Your power to
Forgive insuperable.

Beloved Mother,
What name befits you
Better than paragon of virtues?
Praise be to God,
You accomplished your divine
Mission here on earth .

Your good deeds outlive you,
Time is a great healer,
Time will heal our wounds,
Bye-bye Dear Mother!
May the Good Lord

Welcome you with open arms!

Adieu Mother!
We loved you dearly
We will miss you sorely.
We will remember you
Until we meet again
To part no more.

Armageddon

There is no question!
Few shall live to see
The Day of Judgment.
The pace at which humankind
Is undoing itself bears
Irrefutable testimony.

Yesterday it was the vendetta
Between Rwandan Tutsis and Hutus.
Today it is Armageddon
Between Arafat's suicide bombers
And Ariel Sharon's dogs of war.
Not long ago it was the cold war
Between Yankees and Soviets.

Now it is the feud between Musharraf's
Self-styled freedom fighters
And Vajpayees trigger-happy fanatics.
Yesterday, it was Hamas,
Today it is Boko Haram, al-Shabaab and al-Qaeda
I wonder when humanity will stop
Beating drums of war and courting death.

Other Vistas

Ignorance of other horizons is lethal.
Think of the devastating wars fought
Since the dawn of history,
Root cause is bigotry,
Bigotry breeds prejudice;
Prejudice engenders confrontation.

History is replete with examples.
Think of the holocaust—
Genocide of six million
Jews in Nazi gas chambers,
Think of the Rwandan genocide,
Remember the Persian Gulf War.

Recall the Ethiopia-Eritrean Vendetta,
Don't forget the Libya-Chadian War,
Ponder the Cold War,
Think of Operation Iraqi Freedom
Consider Slobodan's massacres in Bosnia.
The list is interminable.

Sometimes all it takes to avert a full-blown
War is for us to crawl out of our cocoons
And embrace other vistas.
To broaden our horizons
And see the world through new prisms
In order to embrace global peace.

Bravado

I flex my muscles,
I prime my gun;
I pull the trigger
And fire, Poom! Poom!
My foe drops dead
In a pool of blood,
Does that solve my problem?

He that cherishes peace;
Must prepare for war,
There goes the old wives' tale!
Do I have to annihilate
In order to build?
Modus operandi of bellicose nations:
Building in reverse!

Predators

It beggars belief
That man is his own predator.
Take a walk down history.
Revisit the Jewish holocaust.
Have a flashback on
Hiroshima and Nagasaki.

Recall South Africa of Verwoerd;
Bastion of sanctimonious hypocrisy
And social tinkering,
Ponder the harrowing bloodbath
Perpetrated by Hutus against Tutsis
In Rwanda and confines.

Think of Neo-Nazis;
The likes of Idi Amin and ilk,
Relive the nightmare of
September Eleventh in the USA,
All these bear testimony
To man's intolerance of fellow man!

Barrel of the Gun

An armed nation is a safe nation.
These are admonitions
To take with a grain of salt,
Those who declare war do not know
They will perish in war.

The mayhem wrecked
By gun-toting youngsters
In and around school precincts
Bears testimony to the folly that fuels
The craving for firearms in this clime.

Places of learning have become
War zones haunted by delinquents,
Recall Columbine[3],
Remember Sandy Hook[4]
Think of Virginia Tech.[5]

In every nook and cranny,
The specter of death
Hangs over our heads
Like the proverbial
Sword of Damocles.

The media has further
Emboldened these psychopaths
By churning out the hollow
Propaganda that a gun-free
Nation is an unsafe nation.

Witchcraft

Concocted in heathen laboratories,
You pass off as African science.
You're the shame of humanity.
Your evil deeds are plenty,
Permeating all the corners of the globe.

Witchcraft,
A decadent culture.
In your name,
Families are torn apart
In your name.

The young molest the elderly.
In your name,
Houses are burned down at random.
In your name,
Kangaroo courts judge the innocent.

In your name,
The law is flouted with impunity.
Witchcraft,
You pit children against parents.
Because of you,

Sista rises against sista[6].
Because of you, broda rises against broda[7].
You're a stumbling block
To social harmony,
It is time to kiss you farewell!

II. Vice and Virtue

Requiem for Meritocracy

In those good old days
When round pegs stood in round holes,
Meritocracy had signification.
Not anymore!
This is the dawn of a new era—

The reign of mediocrity!
We celebrate mediocrity!
If you desire something done,
You grease my palm.
Nothing goes for nothing—

You scratch my back,
I scratch your own back.
That's the modus operandi.
You want to climb the social ladder?
You'd better gotten yourself a godfather

Or is it a godmother we need?
This is the age of inaptitude.—
Square pegs in round holes.
Sing requiem for meritocracy!
And usher in the reign of mediocrity!

Shenanigans

Unbridled quest for material possessions
Is like a cancer eating deep
Into the bone marrow of our society,
The media is fraught with news about
Shoddy deals, kickbacks and outright theft
By civil servants and individuals.

The incarceration of Inoni Ephraim
At Kondengui came as no surprise to me,
Yves Fotso's meddling in the Albatross Affair
Came as no surprise to me,
The firing of erstwhile Ongolan Ambassador
To Uncle Sam came as no surprise to me.

I'm scandalized by media reports
Concerning compatriots who live in the USA
And continue to earn salaries from Cameroonian
Government coffers for no work done!
Such is the moral bankruptcy
Into which my people have sunk.

Crises

Global cancer
In this day and age
In all nooks and crannies
Is moral crisis—
Graft, half-truths, infidelity
Gerrymandering and fraud.

Corruption,
In all its shapes and colors:
Embezzlement, kickbacks,
Nepotism, cronyism and misappropriation
Are stumbling-blocks to socio-economic
Development and nation-building everywhere.

Corruption breeds instability,
Incapacitates governments,
Alienates foreign investors.
The myopia and imbecility of
Political elites in the Southern Hemisphere
Have reached gargantuan proportions.

Makwerekwere

As pressure mounts on
The Azanian political elite to provide
The rank and file with long-denied amenities,
The rest of Africa will be taken aback
To hear that Azanians of color
Regard other Africans not as fraternal
Brethren who shared their pain
In the Era of apartheid,
But rather as 'makwerekwere.'[8]

This derogatory term qualifies
Foreigners sojourning in South Africa,
Perceived wrongly or rightly as job-snatchers
Conduit of communicable diseases,
Maboya[9] man-hunters and more
It bears stressing that we need
Not over-react to this bushman mentality
My brothers and sisters over there lived in darkness for ages.
Physical darkness has metamorphosed into mental darkness.

The 'makwerekwere' trumpeters
Have been cut off from the rest
Of Africa and the world for too long.
Many of us know a lot about them
But they know us not.
Reason why they don't trust us
In big matters and small
We must strive to bridge the
Gap between THEM and US.

Hullabaloo

Someone is missing the point when
Homosexuals try to equate their
Fate with the predicament of black
Folks in these precincts,
Same-sex marriage is a choice;
And not a civil rights issue.
Blacks didn't have a choice
To be born black or not.

To compare a lifestyle to racism
Is to pool the wool over the eyes of folks!
The black man's greatest enemy is the white
Man in position of power,
Who never utter a racial
Slur in public but would quietly
Do everything in his power to keep
Black folks in perpetual bondage.

Virginity Test

Virginity test,
Scourge of the fair sex.
Intent as an acid test
For sexual probity,
This sleazy ritual
Haunts girls all
Throughout life.

Prime motives:
Halt prenuptial intercourse;
Curb promiscuity,
Is that foolproof?
Sure, virginity restoration
Makes nonsense of
The entire eerie experience!

Worse still, virginity tests aid
The propagation of STDs and AIDS,
The paraphernalia used not sterilized.
Virginity test nothing but a male
Contraption to subjugate
The so-called weaker sex.
Time we sang its requiem!

Kleptocracy

Beware of folks of the underworld!
Day and night they comb
Nooks and crannies of the world
Town, and village on the lookout for loot.
In good weather as in bad,
Day and night, evening and morn,
They leave no stone unturned.

Beware of feymen[10] and feywomen!
In their wake lie countless casualties—
Banks robbed,
Cars burgled,
Homes broken,
Offices ransacked,
Lives terminated at gun-point.

Beware of folks of the underworld!
In their flurry and frenzy
Every weapon comes in handy—
Machete, knife, spear, short-gun,
AK-47 and more.
Mind you kleptomaniac,
Six days for the robber and one day for the owner.

Clando Republic

Clando[1] Republic!
Travesty of a Republic,
They tolerate political mafia,
They refuse to criminalize corruption,
What a state of law!
Your baboons groan,
They yearn for freedom to consume dagga[2]
Your chimpanzees wail,
They moan for freedom to snort cocaine.
Your bitches bark,
They desire freedom to fornicate in public.
Your lions roar,
They desire freedom to drown frustration in jobajo[11].
Your hounds snarl,
They whine about criminalized underage sex.
Your schools are zoos,
Teeming with trigger-happy teens.
Teachers teach in fear,
Learners learn in awe.
This is the dawn of the Jungle Republic,
Vive la République clando![12]

---

[1] clandestine
[2] marijuana

Networking

Networking--
Art of making professional contacts?
Hell No! Not all!
Networking is tantamount
To bribery and corruption!
It's not what you have in your kongolibon[13];
It's who you know.

In Africa,
Folks bribe and corrupt,
White folks network,
Know what I mean?
Networking--
Euphemism for cronyism
And nepotism in the land of white folks.

Networking--
Sobriquet for graft coupled with
Corruption in the land of white folks!
Networking--
Alias for gerrymandering and fraud
In the land of white folks
Networking--

In the Northern Hemisphere,
White folks network,
In the Southern Hemisphere,
Black folks they indulge in
Nepotism and collusion,
That's not networking!

Reckon, there's a difference.

Dirty Linen

Photos of callous sexual assaults
At the Abu Ghraib Prison
Perpetrated by our soldiers
Say much about us as a nation
That pride itself on freedoms.

Horrific scenes at Abu Ghraib
Bring to mind the sexual
Humiliation meted out on
Women by men in uniform
At Denver Post in bygone years.

The inhumanity manifested
At Abu Ghraib by stone-hearted soldiers
Under the gleeful eyes
Of L. England is a replay of the
Daily ordeal meted out at Guantanamo.

We may not know that we
Are washing our dirty linen in public;
The fact of the matter is that
Collectively we are an unclean nation.
That glorifies sadism.

We lie incessantly to ourselves
To the point of believing our own lies
In our daily discourses,
The world is weary
Of our false pretenses!

What if

What if,
Ours were a perfect world,
Megalomaniacs would not
Call the shots left, right and center
Anyhow live and let live.

What if,
Ours were a world without blemish,
Jerks would not
Be Heads of State.
Anyhow, live and let live.

What if,
Our world was a Nirvana
Warmongers would not
Parade themselves as liberators.
Anyhow, live and let live.

What if,
Ours were a sane world
Pedophiles would not
Masquerade as clerics.
Anyhow, live and let live.

What if,
Ours were a humane world
Abortionists would not
Impersonate as pro-lifers.
Anyhow, live and let live.

What if,
Ours were a normal world
Misanthropists would not
Brand themselves philanthropists.
Anyhow, live and let live.

What if,
Ours were a sanctimonious world
Despots would not
Label themselves democrats.
Anyhow, live and let live.

What if,
Ours were a flawless world
Nerds would not
Pass for teachers.
Anyhow, live and let live.

By the way, who are we to judge the world?
One thing for sure, on D-Day,
There will be a tribunal
Where all and sundry will be summoned.
There shall be winners from losers.

Sins of Incumbency

Sins of the incumbency,
Sins of belligerence,
Sins of falsehood,
Sins of prevarication.

The last time we saw
The First Citizen fawning
In the oval office in light-hearted
Mood was during the infamous
Monica Lewinsky Affair.

That was obnoxious enough.
So was Jefferson's lasciviousness.
But there's no comparison
With George's parody on

The reason for waging a
War of mass deception;
Justification for slaughtering
Citizens and denizens
Of an alien land on the basis
Of trumped-up charges!

Vainglory

Amorphous vain monster!
Compulsive obsession
With self-aggrandizement;
Veiled attempt at masking
Innate personal deficiencies.

Whenever vanity pitches home,
Humility seeks refuge on the patio.
Whenever conceit sets foot in a household,
Peace and tranquility cede place
To violence and animosity.

So vile is vanity that he sets
Siblings at daggers drawn.
Pride goes before a fall!
Fools live in fool's paradise
While the wise live on the qui-vive.

Vainglory is man's arch-enemy,
Humanity's nemesis,
Lying in ambush for
Man's ultimate damnation.
Vanity… vainglory… Veneer.

Prevarication

Man and man are locked
In mutual suspicion.
Wife thinks husband is lying.
Husband believes wife is lying.
Child thinks parent is lying.
Parent believes child is lying.

The tax-collector thinks the taxpayer is lying.
The taxpayer believes the tax-collector is lying.
The politician thinks the electorate is lying.
The electorate thinks the politician is lying.
Worse still, the pastor believes the congregation is fibbing
The Pope believes his entourage is lying.

What a load of tall tales!
Tired of hearing these phony tales?
Turn to the Lord for truth!
I am the way, the truth
And the life, Jesus said.
Truthful lips endure forever.

Taximan's Wisdom

Racial prejudice is a skunk!
I call you Nigger!
In mock attempt
At denigration,
In point of fact,
I deride myself.
God doesn't make trash.

You call me coolie!
Blinded by deep-rooted
Bigotry that compartmentalizes
The universe into
Pockets of pigments,
What freaking idiocy!
Mentally retarded you're!

In point of fact,
You live in a fool's
Paradise where
Wisdom is anathema.
You call me Nigger!
My world is built on individualism--

A self-seeking world
Where racial profiling leaves
An indelible mark,
I call you Nigger!
I can't see beyond my nose,
I am a benighted stay-at-home.
I know not who I am…

Disposable Beings

Human trafficking—
The bane of humanity!
Abomination against the human race,
Root causes of this dehumanizing trade?
Greed, materialism, moral decadence!

Main culprits of this inhuman trade—
Expatriates coerced into forced labor
On farms, in factories and in brothels,
The most vulnerable of our society—
Children are not spared the indignity.

Sex trafficking—
The buying and selling of human cargo
For the purpose of sex trade--
Flagrant violation of the Universal
Declaration of Human Rights!

Two million plus persons enslaved
In the global sex industry!
There are more slaves today on
Our land than all the people stolen
From Africa ages ago!

III. Fauna and Flora

Grass

So green
And yet so brown,
Grass
So short
And yet so tall.

Grass is pregnant with meaning,
A myriad aphorisms
Spin around grass.
Grass is always greener
Over the septic tank.

To let grass grow under
Your feet is to procrastinate.
He that has fallen
From grace to grass
Has suffered disgrace.

A green snake in
The grass is a foe;
Not a friend!
Dry grass should never
Play with fire.

Green Rape

On Earth Day year in year out,
We pay lip service to stewardship
Toward the environment,
The worst despoilers make
The loftiest speeches,
Our Environmental Policy Act
Is a loud-sounding nothing!

The Clean Air Act
Is nothing but make-believe,
Not worthier than the
Paper on which it's written,
The Clean Water Act's a sham!
Illegal spills and groundwater
Pollution continues unabated.

We've turned our backs on the Kyoto Treaty,
The prime purpose of which
Is to contain global warming,
We've stalled research on energy efficiency,
Preferring nuclear energy
To solar, wind and other forms
Of alternative energy sources.

Our dirty technologies
Are hazardous to physical
And built environments,
The Land and Water Conservation Fund
Is a white elephant,
Reason why our wetlands

And wildlife habitats are endangered.

In the arena of environmentalism,
Talk is very cheap indeed,
Talk ought to be backed by action.
It's incumbent upon today's tenants
Of the earth to leave to posterity
A better planet than they inherited,
That's common sense!

One Man One Tree

Did you know?
It takes a single
Unlettered man and
One chain saw to demolish
An entire forest.
But it takes an entire village
To plant a single forest!

Trees are our friends,
Indeed our lifeblood.
They have life like we do.
They grow, eat, breathe,
Procreate and die like we do.
Our communion with trees
Must be symbiotic!

And not parasitic,
We need their oxygen;
They need our carbon dioxide.
The more reason
Why our modus vivendi
Should be one man one tree.,
Don't kill fauna and flora!

Earth Poem

You'd be surprised
How many people don't know
That the Earth is fragile.
That's because they don't know
That the ecosystem is a fragile web.

It's amazing
How many people don't know
That natural resources can be depleted.
That's because they don't know
That many of earth's
Resources are non-renewable.

It's mind boggling
How many people don't know
That some of earth's species
Are near extinction.
That's because they don't know
That the earth harbors
A myriad of endangered species.

It's unbelievable
How many people don't know
That Earth's biodiversity
Needs to be protected.
That's because they don't know
That human and green
Capital enjoy reciprocity.

It's unimaginable
How many people don't know
That human beings and the natural
World are on a collision course.
That's because they don' know
That Man's activities often inflict
Irreparable damage to Mother Earth.

It's unfathomable
How many people don't know
That it's incumbent on
The present generation
To meet its needs without
Compromising the ability
Of future generations
To meet their own needs.
That's because they don't know
That we're answerable to posterity.

Ecotage

Wondering what this
Lexis stands for?
It denotes environmental
Terrorism.
Yeah!
We're environmental terrorists.

We terrorize Mother Earth:
Scorch her;
Pollute her;
Suffocate her;
Poison her.
Yeah!

We're Eco-terrorists
We Slash Mother Earth;
Burn her;
Slice her;
Bruise her.
We're are a killer nation!

It is an eyesore.
Streets and parks
Littered with cans, paper,
Bottles, and wrappings.
Aquatic life's choking with litter:
Yeah!

We're green-terrorists
Oil spills;

Toxic waste;
Plastics;
Sewage,
And more!

Biodiversity on the
Brink of extinction.
Wild life endangered
Guess what this generation will
Bequeath to posterity?
A depleted ecosystem!

Crawlers

Myriads of our valued
Friends are crawlers—
Earthworm,
Annelid worm living
And burrowing in the ground.

Millipede,
Anthropod having
A long segmented body
And two pairs of legs
On each segment.

Spider, web-spinning
Eight-legged anthropod having
Round un-segmented body.
Ant, wingless industrious insect
Of the hymenopterous family.

Snail,
Slow-moving gastropod having
A spiral shell
Able to enclose its whole body,
He too is a friend!

Praying mantis,
Insect of the family mantidae,
Holding its forelegs in a
Position suggestive of prayer,
He too is a friend!

Turtle,
Reptile of the order of chelonia,
Encased in a shell of bony plates,
Having webbed toes,
He too is a friend!

A good many of
Our not so good friends
Are crawlers too—
Snake, long limbless reptile
Of the sub-order of ophidia.

Lizard, reptile of the suborder
Of lacertilia, having a long
Body and tail;
Four legs, movable eyelids
And a rough scaly hide.

Gecho,
House lizard having
Adhesive feet for climbing
Surfaces vertically,
These are all friends of nature.

Biodome

The time is 9:00 a.m.
The temperature 65°F.
The date is June 13, 2002
The place Montreal in Canada.

I am in a biodome,
Place devoid of freedom.
There is utter pandemonium.
I am surrounded by a troop

Of elementary and middle schoolers,
Newcomers from all nooks and crannies,
There is nondescript hysteria—
Some are jumping and yelling;

Others are stooping and filming.
Here I am in a dungeon
Meant to steal the freedom
Of man's valued companions—

Amphibians, mammals,
Fishes, reptiles, birds.
I stare in total bewilderment
At this organized chaos—

Self-styled natural environment,
Wondering what on earth these creatures
Have done to deserve
 Such cruel treatment,

Endured without protest,
I can't help but yell:
Injustice done unto one
Is injustice done unto many.

Endangered Species

Humankind and
The natural world
Are locked in a
Collision course.

Our day-to-day
Activities inflict harsh
And often irreparable
Damage to the environment.

Failure to check the current trend
Of human practices
Would put in jeopardy
The survival of generations to come.

And may so alter
The living world that we will be
Unable to sustain
Life hereafter,

Fundamental changes
In attitudes and values
Are desirable if we
Must leave to posterity

A stock of quality
Of life assets no
Less than those we
Have inherited.

The Big Five

It wasn't so much the vast expanse of
Greenery and biotic diversity of the
The Kruger National Park or my face-to-face
Encounter with a live elephant that made the
Longest lasting impression on my five senses.
Rather it was the nocturnal howls of
Famished hyenas that made my hair stand on end.

The Kruger National Park
Is a world of its own,
Harboring a myriad of organisms.
Some visible others microscopic—
First I saw the buffalo;
Then the giraffe;
Later the elephant!

I was dying to see the
Much-acclaimed Big Five:
Leopard, Rhinoceros, Lion, Buffalo, Elephant.
Alas, I ran out of pot-luck.
Nonetheless, a day in the Park
Is worth a lifetime outside.
It's a real African experience!

Snake Sanctuary

This earth is a snake sanctuary
Replete with serpents of all
Shapes and colors—

Rattlesnake,
Poisonous American snake
Of the viperadae family.

Viper, venomous snake
Of the viperadae family;
Python, constricting snake.

Boa constrictor, large nonpoisonous snake
Native to tropical America
And the West Indies;

Fer-de-lance snake,
Highly venomous snake
Native to Central and South America;

Anaconda, large non-poisonous aquatic snake.
With such a multitude of serpents,
How can one play safe?

Camp Fire

What's this word?
Campfires are welcome
Whenever they come.

Campfires are distractions
From our daily attractions.
While we bask in the warmth of a campfire,

We should never misfire
By shooting at the live deer
That lies in good cheer.

The sheer good
Ushered in by a campfire each day
Should be shared by folks every day.

Sounds of Nature

How mute would this world
Be without sounds of nature!
Nature is replete with sounds--
Chirping of insects;
Buzzing of bees;
Croaking of frogs;
Hooting of owls;
Whistling of whales;
Crowing of cocks;
Sizzling of snakes.

Nature is full of sounds--
Barking of dogs;
Mooing of cows;
Squeaking of squirrels;
Mewing of cats;
Roaring of lions;
Trumpeting of elephants;
Bleating of goats;
Crowing of cocks;
Cackling of geeze.

And that's not all—
The snorting of antelopes,
The grunting of camels,
The whooping of monkeys,
The quacking of ducks,
The croaking of frogs,
The chirping of grasshoppers,
The snarling of tigers.

The growling of hippopotamuses,
 The chortling of kangaroos.

Nature abounds with sounds--
Gushing of water;
Pelting of rain;
Cracking of thunder;
Thundering of the earthquake,
These sounds are the life-blood of nature,
Natural sounds complement
Man-made sounds
How dumb would this world
Be without sounds of nature!

Beauty in Nature

There's beauty in nature.
Find happiness in nature.
In the fragrance of flowers,
In the greenery of trees.

There's beauty in nature.
Find glee in nature.
In the rockiness of mountains,
In the stillness of waters.

There's beauty in nature.
Seek comfort in nature,
In the whiteness of snow,
In the brownness of the earth.

There's beauty in nature.
Seek solace in nature,
In the azure of the sky,
In the brightness of the sun.

There's beauty in nature.
Seek tranquility in nature,
In the stillness of night
In the wetness of rain.

There's beauty in nature.
Seek in serenity in nature.
In everything you see.
Go outside and take a look at the moon.

There's beauty in nature.
Enjoy the colors of the rainbow.
Feel the texture of the air.
Smile at the stars.

There's beauty in nature.
Bask in the warmth,
Of the atmosphere.
There's beauty in nature!

Lost Generations

How many more species
Must go extinct
Before it dawns on Man
That he's the worst predator of all times?

Sing requiem for the Dodo,
Sing requiem for the Dinosaur
Sing requiem for White Rhino
Sing requiem for the Black Mamo

Sing requiem for the Hawaiian Akialoa
Sing requiem for the Lanai Creeper
Sing requiem for the Amastra Cornea.
Sing requiem for the Odynerus Radula.

Where is the Dinofelis?
Where is the Metailurus?
Where is the Smilodon?
Where is the Megantereon?

These and many more are
Lost generations whose demise
Is blamed on Man,
Man's actions are a boomerang!

Kola-Nut Tree

Kola nut—
Natural Viagra,
No sexual innuendoes!
Kola nut—
Source of much needed energy--
Energy to perform;
Energy to run;
Energy to walk;
Energy to talk;
Energy to work;
Energy to dance.

Kola nut—
He that brings kola,
Brings life!
Kola nut—
Benevolent companion:
Ingredient in libations;
Part and parcel of bride price;
Pacifier in times of crises,
Kola nut—
African Viagra,
Bedfellow well met!

Brotherhood of the Jungle

I am not a loner.
My siblings are legion:
Lion, king of the jungle;
Tiger, fierce energetic brother,
Leopard, black-potted cousin;
Rhinoceros, thick-skinned plant-eating nephew;
Elephant, gigantic uncle with a trunk and
Long curved ivory tusks;
Buffalo, aunt with backswept horns;
Giraffe, tall niece with a long neck;
Cheetah, swift-running sister with a spotted coat;
Gorilla, large-mouthed stepsister with
Large head and short neck;
Monkey, mischievous mimicking grandma;
Jaguar, choppy flesh-eating grandpa;
Baboon, uncouth stepbrother with a bare butt!

H2O

Water is source of life.
It's also source of many idioms.
To be in deep water,
Is to be in deep trouble,
Still waters that run deep,
Is a quiet manner that
Conceals depths of cunning,
To cast one's bread upon the waters,
Is to do an act of kindness without recompense.

There's more—
Like water off a duck's back,
Is said of remonstrance that
Has no effect.
To make one's mouth water,
Is to stimulate one's anticipation,
Water under the bridge,
Are past events accepted as irreversible.
Water has no enemy.

A fish out of water,
Is said of a person in
An unwelcome situation,
To fish in troubled waters,
Is to take advantage of a bad situation,
Filthy water cannot be washed
Is an African proverb—
We can never know the worth of water
Till the lake is dry.

Christmas Trees

The Christmas tree is a common sight in
The homes of Christians at Christmas,
But what do you do with your tree after Christmas?
If you are like most of the 35 million
Trees-consuming Christians each year,
You haul it to the trash,
Where it will end up in a landfill,
In the process, you are also tossing
Out a variety of benefits the tree
Can offer after the holidays.

The boughs, cut into one-to-two foot lengths,
Can serve as a kind of blanket against
Harsh winter winds for delicate
Perennials such as azaleas, camellias and rosebushes,
The pleasant-smelling needles and cones
Can give a piney aroma to a compost heap,
Although, they take somewhat longer
Than other foliage to decompose,
Evergreens will eventually contribute
To a rich mixture of compost.

Pine and fir needles also make
Good soil conditioners, loosening and
Lightening the consistency of sandy
Or clay soils; the acidic residue they
Give off when they decompose is ideal
For many plants, including azaleas
And rhododendrons; it advisable to add
Some nitrogen to the soil as well because

Decomposing needles can deplete soil nitrogen.
Wise counsel for savvy folks!

The tree trunk can be useful
In the garden, although you'll have
To run it through a shredder or chipper,
The finished product can be added
To the soil as mulch or compost,
Be careful about burning
Evergreens in your fireplace,
The heavy concentrations of resin
Increase the risk of chimney fire,
Besides, the wood burns too quickly to make for a good fire.

Eco-Terrorism

Warfare and a healthy planet are incompatible.
The human species has gone into overdrive
On a growth-obsessed path,
Each year 27,000 species go extinct.
Fresh water sources are drying up.
Microscopic organisms that fertilize
Soil humus is being eradicated.
We're eco-terrorists!

Environmental rights and human
Rights are inseparable:
The ozone hole;
The greenhouse effect;
The extinction of species,
And the predicament of the wretched
Of the eco-system are all interwoven,
We're eco-terrorists!

Life-Savers

You may think of trees as a
Gift from Mother Nature,
Something to climb up or sit under,
Or the cause of fall raking;
You probably don't think of trees as lifesavers.
But that's exactly what they are.

In cities and countryside,
Trees breathe life into our planet
And save us from a host of
Environmental problems;
Aside from the beauty of trees and
The food some of them produce,

Trees are helpful in many ways,
Urban areas are 'heat islands',
Buildings, streets, cars
And other infrastructure,
And human activities soak up heat
On summer days and release it at night.

Researchers have found that average
Temperatures in the city can be five
To nine degrees higher than
Those in surrounding suburbs;
Groups of trees can offset this heat,
Operating as nature's air conditioners.

Trees also help to reduce noise in cities,
Trees offer the cheapest way to

Combat the greenhouse effect by absorbing CO_2
Carbon dioxide is responsible for about
Half of the greenhouse problem
Confronting the global community today.

An average tree absorbs between
26 and 48 pounds of carbon dioxide a year;
An acre of trees takes in about
2.6 tons of carbon dioxide,
Enough to offset the emissions produced
By a car driving 26,000miles.

Trees protect against the
Erosive power of wind,
Helping to protect topsoil
And retain soil moisture.
Deprived of their protective tree cover,
Hillsides are easily eroded

Without trees to break its force,
The wind finds the exposed
Topsoil easy pickings.
Continued wind produces giant,
Gritty clouds that steadily
Diminish precious soil.

The shade provided by trees
Can save considerable amounts
Of energy and money; in the summer,
Three well-placed trees around a house
Can cut home air conditioning energy
Needs by 10 to 15 percent!

Ozone

What is this word?
What's it worth?
Ozone is a colorless reactive gas.
Each molecule of ozone contains
Three oxygen atoms.

At high altitude
These three atoms form
The ozone layer—
Thin layer of the stratosphere,
Rampant use of chlorine-based

Substances namely, chlorofluorocarbons
And chlorinated solvents are the root
Cause of ozone depletion.
The consequences of depletion
Are not obvious to the un-trained eye.

Suffice it to say that before long
Humanity would be grappling
With skin ailments like skin cancer,
Cataracts and more, if nothing is done to halt
The incessant thinning of the ozone layer.

IV. God and Common Good

Summum Bonum

In keeping with the social contract,
The good of one person
Is the good of all and sundry,
It's no good living
On an island like a hermit,
The more the merrier!

The good of one individual
Is the common good,
We are worthy only
In the presence of others,
A wise man once quipped:
Unity is strength.

No man is an island,
Sufficient onto himself,
Seek not the self;
Rather seek the other.
The summum bonum
Bears the seed of universal peace.

Pacifist

An eye for an eye
And a tooth for a tooth!
That's your modus vivendi.
But the Most High has a different
Recipe for you—
Give to Caesar what is Caesar's
And to God what is God's.
Be a pacifist!

Love your enemies.
Do Good to those who hate you,
Bless those who curse you,
Pray for those who mistreat you,
If someone strikes you on one cheek,
Turn to him the other also.
If someone takes your cloak,
Do not stop him from taking your tunic.

Give to anyone who asks you,
And if anyone takes what
Belongs to you,
Do not demand it back.
Do unto others as you would
Have them do to you.
Strive to be a pacifist
In good times and bad times.

Ammo

Christian's secret weapon.
Ask and it will be given to you;
Seek and you will find;
Knock and the door will
Be opened to you.
For everyone who asks receives;
He who seeks finds;
And to him who knocks,
The door will be opened.

The life of Christ on earth was a life of prayer,
The secret of His public ministry
Was His private ministry,
In Heaven His life is one of prayer,
This is the assurance you have
In approaching God—
That if you ask anything
According to His will,
He will answer you.

Prayer—
Secret weapon that helps us recoup
Our strength and energy,
The prayer of a righteous man
Is powerful and effective,
The righteous cry out
And the Lord hears them,
He delivers them from
 All their troubles.

When you pray,
Go into your room.
Close the door and pray
To your Father who is unseen.
Then your Father who sees
What is done is secret,
Will reward you,
Prayer—
Christian's secret weapon.

When we pray
We open the way for the energy
Of God's love to be revitalized in us,
Whatever you ask for in prayer
Believe that you have received it,
And it will be yours.
The Lord is near to all
Who call on Him,
To all who call on Him in truth.

Hand of Friendship

Extend a hand of friendship
To friend and foe alike,
It is the right thing to do.
Forgive those who persecute you,
Forgiveness is a double blessing:
Blesses those that give
And those that receive.

Hold out an olive branch
To those that seek your downfall,
It is the right thing to do.
A tooth for a tooth breeds vengeance.
It is not the right thing to do.
Extend a hand of friendship
To friend and foe alike.

Extend a hand of friendship
To a nagging spouse,
It is the right thing to do.
Two wrongs don't make a right.
Hold out a hand of friendship
To a disgruntled offspring,
It is the right thing to do.

The old may learn from the young;
And the young from the old,
It is the right thing to do.
Extend a hand of friendship
To a begrudging sibling,
It is the right thing to do.

Nurse no rancor.

To err is human
And to forgive is divine.
Hold out a hand of grace
To all and sundry,
It is the right thing to do.
Those who fear the Lord
Are inclined to show brotherly love.

Extend a hand of love to all
Who are created in the image of God,
It is the right thing to do.
A kind word may be charm;
A word may also be harm.
Extend a hand of friendship at all times.
It is the right thing to do.

Deus Caritas Est[14]

God is Love
Dieu est amour[15]
Dios es amor[16]
Mungu ni upendo[17]
Allah shi ne soyayya[18]
Gott ist die Liebe[19]

The River Jordan
Flows into two seas—
Sea of Galilee
With plenty of water and life,
And the Dead Sea,
With no life whatsover.

Are Christians the Sea of Galillee,
Or the Dead Sea?
If we are the Sea of Galilee
Then let God's love flow.
In baptism we received
The gift of love and charity.

If we want to experience,
The love of God
We must be like
The Sea of Galilee.
We must love others;
Even those who seek our downfall.

They know not what they are doing.
Love one another deeply from the heart.

Love comes from God
Hate what is evil.
Cling to what is good.
For God's Love is boundless.

Honor one another.
Whoever loves his brother,
Lives in the light.
And there is nothing
To make him stumble.
God is LOVE.

Everyone who loves has
Been born of God.
Whoever does not love
His brother does not know God.
Love your neighbor as yourself,
For God is love.

God's Rancor

How can God continue to
Bless this tribe of ours?
Come to think of it,
This Society has sent God to quarantine.
Schools are awash with drugs;
Kids misuse guns with impunity;
Teenagers fornicate without qualms.
Marriages are a sham.

Corruption, deceit and self-service,
Unprecedented in our world,
Child molestation and vandalism,
Our stock-in-trade,
Religion now serves as a lethal
Tool for social engineering
This tribe of ours is sick.
Very sick indeed!

Tobasi[20]

Everyone believes
I've charmed my spouse.
Far from it!
The only charm that
Works miracles under
The sun is *LOVE*.

Everyone says
I've given my offspring a potion.
Nothing could be further
From the truth.
The only efficacious tobasi
That I know of is *LOVE*.

Everyone has the conviction
That I've charmed my friends.
Not at all!
My only charm
That works is *LOVE*.
Efficacious tobasi.

Everyone thinks
I've charmed my co-workers.
Never! Ever!
There's only one effective
Charm on earth: *LOVE*.
Strong magan.

Everyone supposes
I've charmed my relatives

Nope! At all!
The only thing that
Works like magic is *LOVE*.
Love is a charm

LOVE is Tobasi
LOVE is Magan[21]
LOVE is a talisman.
Give it without regard
To race, age, gender or creed
It works like Famla![22]

Time

There's time for everything—
Time to be born and time to die,
Time to plant and time to uproot,
Time to tear down and time to build.

There's time to weep and time to laugh,
Time to mourn and time to dance,
Time to smile and time to frown,
Time to be quiet and time to speak up.

There's time to embrace and time to refrain,
Time to search and time to give up,
Time to keep and time to throw away,
Time to bully and time to be subservient.

There's time to tear and time to mend,
There's time to love and time to hate,
Time for war and time for peace,
But God's time is the best!

Same Boat

The same fate awaits all men.
As one man dies, so dies the other.
All have the same breath,
All have the same red blood.
No man has an edge over
His neighbor in God's eyes,
Before God all earthly
Possessions ill-gotten or not,
Are totally worthless.

We're all in the same boat;
From dust we all come,
Unto dust we will all return.
Who knows if the spirit of one man
Rises and the spirit of the
Other goes down into the earth?
So there's no better way for men
To live than to enjoy their companionship
In the fellowship of the holy spirit.

Before God,
There's no Docta[23],
No Professor,
No President,
No General,
No PDG
No élu du peuple![24]
No chief
No nchinda!

Shepherd

The Lord is my Shepherd.
He is my Shield, Protector and Deliverer.
He's the good Shepherd.
He has the heart of a shepherd,
Beating with pure, generous love.

The Lord is my Shepherd.
He has the eye of a shepherd.
He has the faithfulness of a shepherd.
He has the strength of a shepherd.
He has the tenderness of a shepherd.

But there's more—
My Shepherd laid down His life for me.
He bore my sins for me.
The word 'shepherd' bears
Thoughts of tenderness.

Flock

Suffer little children
Come unto me.
They are God's children.
They make up the Flock.

Suffer gays
Come unto me.
They are God's children.
They make up the flock.

Suffer lesbians
Come unto me.
They are God's children.
They make up the flock.

Suffer whores
Come unto me.
They are God's children.
They make up the flock.

Suffer pedophiles
Come unto to me.
They are God's children.
They make up the flock.

Suffer dipsomaniacs
Come unto to me.
They are God's children.
They make up the flock.

Suffer drug addicts
Come unto to me.
They are God's children.
They make up the flock.

To err is human;
To forgive is divine.
I came not to save the righteous
But the unrighteous, says the Lord.

Marble

Under every dark cloud
There is a silver lining.
Humankind has got much
To be grateful for,
We'd do better to count
Our blessings
Rather than brood
Over petty failures.

Life is not a bed of roses.
There's no rose
Without a thorn,
Inordinate ambition seems to be
Man's very demolition.
Let's slow down now
And make room for God
In our lives now.

Fear of God
Is the beginning of wisdom,
He that banks on bread alone
Is doomed to fail,
There are no easy rides in life.
It's a long haul,
This life of ours,
Everyone pays a due.

Slow down now!
Rome wasn't built in a day
Nor did Michelangelo script

'The David' in a day!
He spent years breathing life into marble.
Life is a marble,
We've got to chisel away
And pare it down to its essence.

Lord's Face

Wherefore these fights and
Quarrels among you?
They come from desires that
Battle within you,
You villainous people!

Don't you know that friendship
With the world is tantamount to
Friendship with God?
You desire something but you don't get it.
You kill in order to get what you covet.

You quarrel and fight,
You slander one another!
Anyone who speaks against his
Brother speaks against God.
God opposes the proud

Therefore, submit yourselves to God,
Wash your soiled hands,
Purify your stony hearts,
Humble yourselves before God
And he will lift you up!

Servants of Satan

Woe unto those who call evil
Good and good evil.
Woe unto those who take darkness
For light and light for darkness.
Woe unto those who take bitter
For sweet and sweet for bitter!

And woe unto those who are wise
In their own eyes
And clever in their own sight,
Woe unto those that are heroes at
Drinking liquor and champions
In fornication!

And woe unto those who acquit
The guilty for a bribe but
Deny justice to the innocent.
Their roots will decay
And their flowers will
Blow away like dust.

Wrong Way!

This land is on the brink of
A moral catastrophe.
There's no faithfulness,
No love of neighbor,
No acknowledgement of God.
There's only cursing, addiction, murder,
Prevarication, larceny and adultery.

Bloodshed follows bloodshed.
Atonement cannot be made
For the land on which blood has been shed,
When you defile the graves
Of ancestors with the blood of
Your brethren, calamity befalls you.
This is the law of Karma!

The land mourns its youth
Cut down in their prime of life!
All those who live on it waste away.
They stumble day and night.
For want of knowledge,
The people who live on this land will be destroyed.
There's not one righteous man on this land,
Not even one! Not one!

There's not one who understands divine ways,
Not one who seeks God.
All have turned away,
They have together become villains.
There's not one who does good.

Their throats are like open graves.
Their tongues practice deceit.
The poison of vipers is on their lips.

Their mouths are full of swearing,
Words of spitefulness,
They are swift to
Demand a pound of flesh,
Vengeance is their hallmark,
Ruin and misery trail their footprints,
The way of peace they do not know,
This land is on the verge of a major cataclysm.

V. People and Praise

Baobab

[Tribute to my departed father
Unsung hero of Teuloh Quarter in Bamunka,]

Lion man,
I salute you in the world yonder.
Out of sight but not out of mind,
Unparalleled in prowess
Unmatched in valor,
Your name—buzz word in the village.

Lion man,
Humble yet indomitable,
You defied all man-made constraints.
Unlettered but educated,
You left no stone unturned
In a bid to nurture your offspring.

Fallen Baobab,
Be gleeful in your new abode,
Your dreams have come true,
Hither and thither,
Your name resonates.
Your progeny is legion.

True son of the soil,
Generous with praise,
Slow to anger,
Magnanimous in many ways ,
Prosperous is your progeny,
Long is your genealogy.

Should you return this day,
You'd be awed by the growth
Of the seeds you planted.
Adieu Daddy,
Bye, Bye Bobo!
Until we meet again.

Sweet Mother

Affection incarnate,
Symbol of the genteel,
Unlettered yet suave,
Sweet mother!

You gave me the light of day,
You nursed me in good times and bad.
You nurtured me from infancy
To full-blown adulthood.

You're priceless, sweet mother.
You may not be flawless,
Foibles being integral to human condition,
Yet, you're the quintessence of motherhood.

Robbed of your better by the stealthy thief,
The omnipresent hawk,
You stopped at nothing,
To fulfill your parental DUTY.

 Mother of one and mother of all,
Here is my song of gratitude to you.
How can I repay your toil other than
Love you in even in death?

Demise of a Virtuoso

[Tribute to Mongo Beti, celebrated Cameroonian
writer who died on October 8, 2001]

Mongo Beti is dead!
Long live Mongo Beti!
Cameroon's virtuoso of letters
Porte-parole of the voiceless,
Mouth-piece of *Les Damnés de la terre*[25]
Succumbed to the iron fist
Of death on that fateful day .
His was a losing battle
Against a cancerous kidney;
His fall akin to the tumble
Of a baobab eaten up by white ants.

But death be not so proud!
Mongo Beti is dead but lives on,
His verbal artistry immortalizes.
You've numbed his voice;
Yet his vocal plume speaks.
You've blinded him;
Yet his literary legacy sees.
You've cut his breath;
Yet his masterpieces breathe.
From the ashes of Mongo
Shall surge forth a great many Betis.

In Memoriam

[Tribute to the Obasinjom Warrior]

Wheda you be bookman
Or you be half-book man.
Wheda you be teacher
Or you be na school pikin.
Wheda you be man
Or you be na woman
Wheda you be small man
Or you be na big man.
I mimba say you sabe that 'shooting star'
Wey them de call'am say Bate Besong.
That man na alagata pepper for Cameroon.

Forseka yi book,
Plenty pipo them like BB.
Forseka yi book,
Plenty pipo them badhart BB.
Some pipo them say BB
He book na djindja[26]
Other one them say

BB yi book na daso cush fullup for inside.
BUT make I tell wuna something:
The thing wey yi de worry pipo them for BB
Yi book na daso de true tok wey yi de tok'am.

Una sabe say lie man yi badhart
Man wey yi de tok true tok
ME,
I like BB.
BB na strong bookman,
BB na man wey yi di tok true tok,
BB na man wey yi no de fia yi some man.

Na one thing that wey yi make I de sing
This ma own song for BB, aka Obassijom Warrior!

So no, I say BB dong bolè,

But long live BB!

Tribute to a mentor
[at the Defense Language Institute-Monterey, California]

Chief Bokde,
Indefatigable role-player,
Slow to anger,
And quick to correct,
Fired by zeal to accomplish,
Unfazed by the gargantuan workload at SLC[27],
Your sterling legacy lives on.

Chief Bokde,
Genuine intellectual,
Committed to mission accomplishment,
Amiable colleague,
Admirable supervisor,
You're a role model.

Chief Anand,
Had we the means,
We'd clone you,
Had we the might,
We'd replicate you,
Had we the power,
We'd keep you.

Alas,
We must say—
Adieu!
Goodbye!
Au revoir!
¡hasta la vista!

Heroes of Africa

Hail Mother Africa!
Hail heroes of Africa!
From the Cape to Cairo,
They are legion—
Nelson Mandela,
Winnie Madikizela-Mandela,
Wangari Maathai,
Thomas Sankara,
Patrice Lumumba,
Kwame Nkrumah,
Leopold Sedar Senghor,
Julius Nyerere,
Ahmed Sékou Touré,
Jomo Kenyatta,
Samora Machel,
Kofi Atta Annan
Muammar Gaddafi,
Robert Mugabi.
These illustrious sons
And daughters of Africa
Have done us proud!
Alas, every rose has its thorns-
From the ashes of alien dictators,
Have arisen home-grown dictators—
Yesterday, it was Jean Bedel Bokassa,
The cannibalistic despot
Of Central African Republic.
Yesterday, it Haile Selassie Mariam,
Today, it is Daniel Arap Moi,
The powerful megalomaniac of Kenya.

Yesterday it Hastings Kamuzu Banda of Malawi,
Today it is blood-thirsty Sani Abacha of Nigeria.
Not long ago it was Ahmadou Ahidjo,
The sanctimonious Moslem hypocrite of Cameroon,
Today it is Paul Biya,
The voiceless eunuch from Mvo-Meka.
Not long ago, it was Idi Amin Dada of Uganda,
Nowadays, it is the numskull Yoweri Museveni
The architect of no-party democracy!
Yesterday it was Dawda Kairaba Jawara,
Today, it is the lunatic doctor-cum-professor semi-literate
Yahya Abdul-Aziz Jemus Junkung Jammeh
Who decides the fate of Gambians
The list of Africa's anti-heroes is long-
Mobutu Sese Seko of Zaire,
Samuel Doe of Liberia,
Blaise Compaore of Burkina Faso,
Hosni Mubarak of Egypt,
Zine El Abidine Ben Ali of Algeria
Uhuru Kenyetta of Kenya,
Teodoro Obiang Nguema Mbasogo
Of Equitorial Guinea
Idriss Debby of Chad...
Beware brothers and sisters of Africa,
The heroes of today,
 May become the dictators of tomorrow!

Kudos!

What's in a name?
Not a rhetorical interrogation!
The nomenclature 'Steven Winspur'
Is literally and metaphorically
Pregnant with significations—
Lexicographers align the signifier 'Steven'

With sexiness, adroitness, suaveness, sophistication
Steven: attractive physically and mentally too!
What's in the name Winspur?
Old Anglo-Saxon personal name associated with
Joy, friendship, perspicacity, pro-action
Professor Steven Winspur was all of that and more—

Passionate teacher, sagacious mentor,
Guarantor of sacrosanct values of academe,
Dependable conduit of knowledge,
Indefatigable crusader in defense of academic freedom,
Above all, a real gem in the ivory tower of literati,
Good fortune brought me under the aegis

Of this fine academic in the Fall of 2004,
When I enrolled into the doctoral Program at UW-Madison
Steven nurtured me with carrot and stick
Throughout the entire rite of passage
Until I gained admission into the PhD Hall of Fame in 2009,
To Steven, I say *mille fois merci pour un travail bien accompli!*

Better Half

Apple of my eye,
You surpass all epithets,
You aren't superhuman
Yet you have carved out a niche
Deep down in my heart of hearts.

Apple of my eye,
You're so special,
Your deep sense of humor humbles me.
Your humility overshadows your petty flaws.
You're an iconic better half!

Apple of my eye,
You're a paragon of virtues,
You exude confidence,
And inspire true love.
These words, my LOVE are a tribute to you.

VI. Power and Politics

Double-Speak

On election day,
They promised good roads;
Instead we got death-traps.
On voting day,
They promised an end to Chômercam[28];
Instead we got chronic unemployment.
On election day,
They guaranteed us free education;
Instead we got shopping mall education.
On voting day,
You promised well equipped hospitals;
Instead we got human abattoirs.
On election day,
They promised a crime-free society;
Instead we got a crime-ridden country.
On voting day,
They promised rigor and morality;
Instead we got rancor and immorality.
On election day,
They promised transparency
And accountability;
Instead we got graft and corruption.
On voting day
They promised a rosy life for all;
Instead we got perpetual penury.
On that day,
When they shall come again with tall tales
We shall no longer gobble
Down their prevarications,
Hook, line and sinker.

When that day comes
For them to canvass for our ballots,
We'll look them in the face,
And say: you're chameleons,
On vous connaît![29]
Fuck off! One good turn
Deserves another.

Pseudo-Democrats

In these precincts,
Polls are seldom a litmus test
For popular mandate,
Benefiting from the privilege
Of incumbency the powers-that-be
Make a sham of fair and free ballot.

The legislature transformed
Into a rubberstamp;
The judiciary reduced to the posture
Of a toothless bulldog,
The execute lords it over,
By fair means and foul!

For this self-same reason
Pundits have branded
Our brand of democracy
brazen demo-craziness!
A befitting nomenclature
For our *démocratie à la camerounaise.*[30]

Rape of Democracy

Did I hear democracy?
Me thought I thought I heard demo-craziness.
To perpetuate your stay in power,
You resort to unholy contraptions.
The modus operandi of your game is foul play.
The end justifies the means, you say.
Might is right, you chant.
Machiavelli, you're.
You rape democracy
And flout laws.
Democracy and fair game are strange
Bedfellows in your lexicon.
Democracy *à la votre* is a sham.
Totalitarianism and pluralism are antithetical.
Who's fooling who?
That's the question!

You think you can
Fool all the people all the time?

Our clime is saddled with militarized democracies
Sickened to the marrow by junta regimes.

Their stewardship riddled with coups.
In your demo-craziness you muzzle the press
And give leeway to electoral fraud
And gerrymandering.

Your demo-crazy is malignant
Your demo-craziness is counterproductive.

It stifles talent,
It silences dissenting voices.

Démocracie à l'ongolaise[31]
It violates fundamental rights and freedoms
It is a mockery of democracy
It belongs in the trashcan of underachievers.

Hellhole

The people christen you Unity Palace
Yet you're a house full of shit,
The rank and file brand you Etoudi,
Yet you're a hell-hole,
Presidential palace?
That's a misnomer!

Behind your glitter and glamor,
Lurk many a machination.
Behind your shaded curtains
Linger many a shady deal.
Dog-eat-dog is your modus operandi.
In that shithouse of yours.

I shed tears for Irène,
I mourn Baba Toura,
I empathize with Ephraim Inoni,
I have no tolerance for the Ashawo
Who has metamorphosed into *Première Dame*!
What disrespect for a respectable nation!

I wear sackcloth for the victims of April 6.
I put emblematic wreaths on their unknown tombs.
Have you laid their ghosts to rest?
Have you washed your hands clean of their blood?
I smell incest and adultery at Etoudi,
Perversion is the stock-in–trade of your cabal.

Many have perished in your macabre name
Others sent to Kondengui to save face death.

What load of bullshit!
Pa Paul, that Kondengui
Ndamba équipe[32] will never be
Complete until you join them.

Not long from now.
Those who feed crocodiles with human heads
Will be fed to crocodiles, make no mistake.
You may run but you won't hide
On vous connaît tous! We know you all!

Watch out,
Tenant of Etoudi,
Fon of Fons of Etoudi,
Roi-fainéant of Etoudi,
He that kills by the sword,
Dies by the sword!

Phoenix

Election Américaine 2012—[33]
Véritable vendetta![34]
I saw David pitted against Goliath,
I saw the clash of bigotry with magnanimity.
I saw the triumph of altruism over egocentrism.
Election Américaine 2012—
Véritable combat des géants!
I heard the raucous cacophony of an owl
Drown by the sweet lyrics of a phoenix.
I heard the debilitating rant of myopia
Muted by the melodious chant of perspicacity.

Election Américaine 2012—
Véritable guerre sans pitié[35]
Merciless tug of war!
I saw indigence at daggers drawn with opulence.
I saw humility at loggerheads with superciliousness.
I saw veracity fighting tooth and nail against prevarication.
Election Américaine 2012—
Lutte à qui mieux mieux![36]
Cut-throat duel!
I smelt the triumph of Light over Darkness.
I sensed the victory of a Messiah
Over the Waterloo of Judas.
Election Américaine 2012
I witnessed the landslide of Majority over Minority.
I witnessed the triumph of Black over White.
Black and Proud!
Not the Wretched of the Earth anymore.
Election Américaine 2012

Never say never again!
Fools walk where angels
Dread to tread
Others live in fool's paradise.
Election Américaine 2012

Goliath reduced the Battle
To bread and butter,
David saw it as a civil rights matter—
America with liberty and justice for ALL!
Election Américaine 2012
From 'loser' to Winner!
From He that leads from behind
To Commander-in-Chief!
From One-Term to Two-Term President,
Grand return of the Phoenix to the White House!

VII. Pen and Penmanship

Barrel of the Pen

A bazooka shots to kill,
My pen writes to annihilate.
Like a bulldozer it levels
All minutiae in its trail—
Graft, perversion, ineptitude,
Corruption, nepotism, cronyism,
Promiscuity, impunity, feymania
Gravy train, gerrymandering and ilk.

A canon booms to exterminate,
My plume resonates to kill.
No one escapes unscathed.
It has scores to settle with
All and sundry,
In all nooks and crannies,
In high places and in the lowly
Man, woman and child.

A missile detonates,
To hit every target in its orbit,
My pen blasts to lambaste
Butts left, right and center.
It's no respecter of social
Rank or economic standing,
It's the voice of the voiceless.

Penmanship

I write what I want
Writers are born; not made
That's an old wives' tale.
He that has nothing to say can't write.
Quips George Bernard Shaw

Penmanship like all trades
Is cultivated,
It's product of fine schooling.
It's got nothing to do with hacking
It does not tally with plagiarism

Pen-pushing,
Is an art
It abhors mimicry;
And frowns on mediocrity
This is not a figment of my imagination!

Poetry

I write verse therefore I am.
Poets are not dead wood
As many make us believe.
Versification is a vehicle for the
Transportation of mixed emotions.

Poets create their own world;
World as it should be.
Poetry stands for a worldview.
Poetry performs a myriad of social functions—
How reverent the lyrics of our Anthem!

Isn't that poetry?
How soul-searching the melody of our hymnals!
Isn't that poetry too?
How captivating our rhymed commercials!
That too is poetry!

Poetry is not dead wood.
It's a showcase of verbal artistry,
Genre in its own right.
Vive la poésie![37]
Long Live Poetry

Poetic License

Screw this asteroid!
I wanna say what I gotta say
No motherfucker's gonna
Tell me to shut the fuck up!
The underworld has put
Every dick in dipshit.
This gives me the creeps.

This joint's gone bunkers!
Bunch of dirtballs have
Hijacked no man's land
What do ya make of that one, dude?
Say they're slaughtering in Tonton[38] Sammy's name!
That's a load of crap, don't ya think?
Thou shall not kill
Is the first law in God's BIG book.
Yet servants of satan kill in God's name.

These dirt-bags
Are darned assholes
Say we're a cocky self-serving nation.
Cold fact is they're pissed
Off at our self-styled freedoms:
Freedom to cheat, steal and fib
According to our freaking consciences.

Nom de Plume

The euphoria is nondescript!
I'm at a loss for words
To qualify the glee that overwhelms me
Each time I see my *nom de plume* in print

It's a renewed feeling of accomplishment
That floods my heart of hearts
Each time I catch a glimpse of
My brainchild in print.

The glee that comes with triumph over
The rejection slip is unknown
To those who have never
Put pen to paper!

Sharks and materialists
Count their wealth in gold and diamond;
I count my opulence in penmanship.
I pride myself on scholarship.

VIII. Dribs and Drabs

Blackman's Burden

What's the hullabolloo
About being black?
Why do we take delight in
Ascribing pejorative connotations
To the color black?

Black market is illicit
Traffic in contraband goods.
Black mass is a travesty of
The Roman Catholic Mass.

Black sheep of a family
Is a disreputable
Member of the family
Black magic is magic involving
Supposed invocation of evil spirits!

Black Maria is a police vehicle
For transporting prisoners,
Black economy is unofficial economics.
Black Death is a widespread
Epidemic of bubonic plague.
Ad infinitum!

Secret Number

SSN
Social Security Number,
So trivial and yet so weighty,
Indispensable to natives,
Invaluable to alien residents.

SSN
Master key to every form of
Employment in these precincts—
White-collar like blue-collar.
It knows no bounds.

SSN
Password for every form of
Bureaucratic transaction nationwide,
Ubiquitous magic number,
Life-blood of all wheeling and dealing.

SSN
Alias for passport to
Social security in Uncle Sam.
No one is any one
Without the SSN.

Hearthstone

625 West Prospect Avenue
Stoops the Centenarian,
Hearthstone erected in 1882,
Replica of Victorian ornate architecture.

Hearthstone—
Landmark in Fox Valley Heritage,
Enjoys pride of place in the
Register of National Monuments.

Hearthstone—
Cradle of modern electric energy;
Home of Henry James Rogers,
Appleton erstwhile magnate.

September 30, 1882
Hearthstone became the first
House in the world to be lighted
By hydroelectric energy.

Powered by the Edison 'K' dynamo.
Appletonians[39] woke up to find
Hearthstone illuminated by
A central hydroelectric station.

Today, Hearthstone stands on
The brink of decrepitude owing
To time-induced wear and tear;
Much to the chagrin of friends of Hearthstone.

Fox Cities

April 21, 1857—
Birthday of present-day Appleton[40],
Christened after Samuel Appleton.

Appleton—
Nexus of the Fox Cities—
Neenah, Menasha, Kaukauna.

Fox Cities—
Epithet for communities
Clustered around Appleton—

Kimberly, Little Chute, Combined Locks,
Greenville, Grand Chute, Center,
Freedom, Vanderbrock, Buchanan, Harrison.

A walk down memory lane,
Dates Fox Cities back to the Menominee—
Nation within the Nation—

Wild Rice Eaters,
Descendants of the great bears—
Wisconsinites a.k.a Fox Indians.

Restroom

The hustle-and-bustle
Of our time makes the
Presence of the restroom alias latrine
In every nook and cranny of
The vicinity a welcome relief.

Hard pressed folks have recourse
To the restroom not only
To jettison human waste
But also to stave off the
Travails of mundane world.

Curiosity!
Demented folks resort
To the restroom to vent
Their spleen in the form
Of obscene graffiti.

Bubble Mentality

Wholesome views about the rest
Of the world cannot be acquired
By people who vegetate in little corners
Of the globe like hermits for eternity,
To do so would be tantamount
To enshrouding ourselves
In bubble mentality,
A.K.A black bush mentality.

Bubble mentality confines us
To the belief that nothing is more
Important than where we are
And who we are,
Travel is fatal to this kind
Of myopic worldview,
And many of us need it sorely.
Time to get rid of black-bush mentality!

Slanguage

What's this brouhaha
About alien accents?
Who the heck knows what you mean
When you say 'bubbler' for water fountain?

What's this hullabaloo
About strange accents?
Who in the world knows what you mean
When you say 'I betcha'?

What's this raving and ranting
About foreign accents?
Which son of a gun knows what you mean
When you say 'you bet'?

What's this rowdiness
About strong accents?
Who around knows what you mean
When you say 'y'all'?

What's this hubbub about
Language slaughter ?
Who in the vicinity knows what you mean
When you say 'soda' for pop and 'Pop' for soda?

Need we really whine about
Speech idiosyncrasies?
When we run around saying'It's my bad'
To mean 'it's my mistake'?

You Name It!

There's nothing more important
Than a person's name.
The problem is we toy around with names.
People no longer use their real names!
We take liberties with nomenclature:

Elizabeth has become Beth;
Susan has metamorphosed into Sue;
Patricia has been reborn Pat or Patty;
Christopher has been transformed into Chris;
Michael is Mike.

Charles is Chuck,
Peter is Pete,
And the list continues.
Why are we doing this?
We make others feel like human counterfeits!

Do you know what's done
To people who have tongue-twisting names
Like Shosholoza?
We ignore them altogether?
Isn't that smart!

People's names are their most
Valued assets from birth,
We have no leeway to
Trifle with people's names!

Notes

[1] Police man

[2] Royal pages

[3] The Columbine High School massacre was a school shooting that occurred on April 20, 1999, at Columbine High School in Columbine, an unincorporated area of Jefferson County in the state of Colorado. The perpetrators, two senior students Eric Harris and Dylan Klebold, murdered a total of 12 students and one teacher. They injured 21 additional people, while attempting to escape the school. The pair then committed suicide.

[4] The Sandy Hook Elementary School shooting occurred on December 14, 2012, in Newtown, Connecticut, when 20-year-old Adam Lanza fatally shot 20 children and 6 adult staff members. Prior to driving to the school, Lanza shot and killed his mother at their Newtown home. As first responders arrived at the scene, Lanza committed suicide by shooting himself in the head.

[5] The Virginia Tech shooting (also known as the Virginia Tech massacre) was a school shooting that took place on April 16, 2007, on the campus of Virginia Polytechnic Institute and State University in Blacksburg, Virginia, United States. Seung-Hui Cho, a senior at Virginia Tech, shot and killed 32 people and wounded 17 others in two separate attacks, approximately two hours apart, before committing suicide.

[6] Sister

[7] Brother

[8] Derogatory term for foreigner

[9] Prostitute

[10] Conmen

[11] Beer

12 Long live Clando Republic!

13 Close-shaven head

14 God is love in Latin

15 God is love in French

16 God is Love in Spanish

17 God is love in Swahili

18 God is love in Hausa

19 God is love in German

20 Charm

21 Talisman

22 Secret society

23 Doctor

24 People's representative

25 Reference to Franz Fanon's book of the same title

26 Hard to understand

27 Student Learning Center at the Defense Language Institute

28 Unemployment in Cameroon

29 We know you well

30 Cameroon-styled democracy

31 Ongola is Owondo name for Yaoundé.

32 Soccer team

33 2012 Election in America

34 True vendetta

35 Merciless war

36 Cut throat contest

37 Long Live Poetry

38 Uncle

39 Inhabitants of the city of Appleton in Wisconsin

40 City in the State of Wisconsin, USA

Printed in the United States
By Bookmasters